PASSIONS...

Skiing

PASSIONS...

Skiing

PHOTOGRAPHS SUPPLIED BY SKISHOOT–OFFSHOOT

DREAM PLACES YOU'D RATHER BE

DUNCAN BAIRD PUBLISHERS

LONDON

PASSIONS... *Skiing*

First published in the United Kingdom and
Ireland in 2005 by
Duncan Baird Publishers Ltd
Sixth Floor
Castle House
75–76 Wells Street
London W1T 3QH

Conceived, created and designed by
Duncan Baird Publishers

Managing Editor: Kirsten Chapman
Managing Designer: Manisha Patel
Picture Researcher: Louise Glasson

British Library Cataloguing-in-Publication Data:
A CIP record for this book is available from the
British Library

ISBN-10: 1-84483-173-6
ISBN-13: 9-781844-831739

10 9 8 7 6 5 4 3 2 1

Typeset in Bergell and Futura
Colour reproduction by Colourscan, Singapore
Printed in Singapore by Imago

HOUSTON
MILES
C.B.
MANILA 8199 MI
PHOENIX 1210 MI
GREENLAND 220
Fretter, Germany 7293 km
ANCHORAGE 1387 MI

Foreword

I'VE BEEN SKIING SINCE I WAS TWO, AND EARLY IN MY LIFE IT BECAME MY PORTAL TO ANOTHER WORLD. THE MOUNTAINS WERE A PEACEFUL PLACE, WHERE I COULD GET AWAY FROM PARENTS, SCHOOL, AND THE OBLIGATIONS OF LIFE. AS I GREW OLDER I CAME TO APPRECIATE THESE TIMES MORE AND MORE. IF EVER I HAD A BAD DAY, SKIING WOULD SOMEHOW MAKE THINGS RIGHT (EVEN SITTING ON THE CHAIR-LIFT COULD SETTLE MY THOUGHTS). ONCE ON MY SKIS I COULD ROAM THE THREE-DIMENSIONAL WORLD OF THE MOUNTAINS, FREE AS A FISH IN THE SEA.

SINCE THE SPORT'S BEGINNINGS, IT HAS BEEN ASSOCIATED WITH PICTURES AND FILMS. WHEN I WAS YOUNG MY BEDROOM WAS COVERED WITH SKI POSTERS WHICH INSPIRED MY DREAMS. AND SKI FILMS HAVE NOW BECOME A HUGE PART OF THE LIFESTYLE. IT WAS IN THE FILM "SKI THE OUTER LIMITS" THAT I HEARD BARRY CORBET DESCRIBE THE SPORT AS THE "CONQUEST OF THE USELESS". TAKE AWAY ALL THE GIBBERISH OF TECHNIQUE AND EQUIPMENT, AND SKIING IS SIMPLY A WONDERFUL WAY OF SPENDING YOUR TIME – A SPORT THAT'S

ENJOYED ACROSS THE GLOBE BY PEOPLE OF ALL
AGES, ABILITIES, AND WALKS OF LIFE.

AND WHEN YOU'RE IN SKI COUNTRY, ALL
LANGUAGES BECOME ONE. I ONCE SPENT A WEEK IN
ITALY'S DOLOMITES WITH A FRIEND OF A FRIEND
WHOM I HAD NEVER MET. WE HAD LITTLE MORE THAN
"YES" AND "NO" IN OUR SHARED VOCABULARY, BUT
WE GOT ALONG FINE. I'VE ALSO BEEN FORTUNATE
ENOUGH TO SPEND TIME IN JAPAN, WHERE MY LACK
OF JAPANESE HAS NEVER HELD ME BACK – SMILING
FACES NEED NO TRANSLATION.

AS YOU LOOK THROUGH THIS BOOK, I HOPE
YOU ARE TAKEN AWAY FROM WHERE YOU ARE TO A
PLACE WHERE YOU NEED TO BE. LET THE IMAGES
TAKE YOU TO THE MOUNTAINS, WHERE YOU CAN
ENJOY TIME BY YOURSELF OR WITH FRIENDS OR
FAMILY, CHASING THE CONQUEST OF THE USELESS.

GLEN PLAKE

"The secret of reaping the greatest enjoyment from life is to live dangerously!"

FRIEDRICH NIETZSCHE (1844–1900)

"How glorious a greeting the sun gives the mountains!"

JOHN MUIR (1838–1914)

"Today a new sun rises for me; everything is alive, everything is energized, everything seems to speak to me of my passion, everything asks me to cherish it."

NINON DE L'ENCLOS (1620–1705)

"It is not because things are difficult that we do not dare, it is because we do not dare that they are difficult."

"For strong souls
Live like fire-hearted suns;
to spend their strength
In furthest striving action."

GEORGE ELIOT (1819–80)

"The time available to us
every day is elastic;
the passions we feel
can lengthen it ..."

MARCEL PROUST (1871–1922)

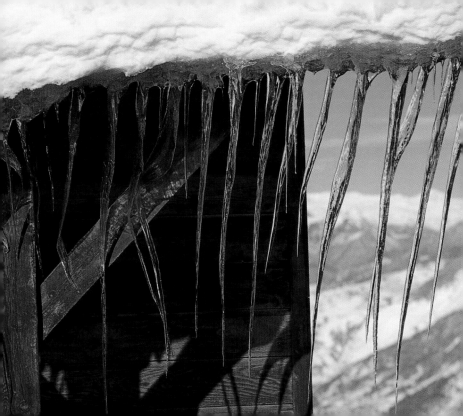

"... silent icicles,
Quietly shining to the quiet
moon."

SAMUEL TAYLOR COLERIDGE (1772–1834)

"Bouncing, floating lightly in impossibly soft powder, you lose and find yourself."

VICKI NIELSON

"When you look at life
from a mountain top,
you see no limitations;
there is simply immensity."

HAZRAT INAYAT KHAN (1887–1927)

"There is nothing in the world more beautiful than the forest clothed to its very hollows in snow. It is the still ecstasy of nature ..."

WILLIAM SHARP (1855–1905)

"Powder snow skiing is not fun. It's life, fully lived, life lived in a blaze of reality."

DOLORES LA CHAPELLE

"Soaring along the line between fear and sheer joy, we find moments of purest inspiration."

ROBERT FLORES (1919–2000)

"If you're not living on the edge, you're taking up too much space."

PROVERBIAL WISDOM

"The splendor of silence —
of snow-jeweled hills
and of ice."

INGRAM CROCKETT (1856–1936)

"The sensual caress of waist-deep cold smoke .... [They] glory in skiing virgin snow, in being the first to mark the powder with the signature of their run ..."

TIM CAHILL

"When I let go of what I am,
I become what I might be."

LAO TZU (3RD–4TH CENTURY BC)

"Go confidently in the direction of your dreams. Live the life you've imagined."

HENRY DAVID THOREAU (1817–62)

"I am here to live out loud."

EMILE ZOLA (1840–1902)

"In the middle of a crowd,
I feel the peace of the
mountains."

NATIVE AMERICAN POEM

"Great things are done when men and mountains meet."

WILLIAM BLAKE (1757–1827)

Locations

About the contributors

GLEN PLAKE, FOREWORD

With his trademark hairstyle (a colourful mohican), Glen Plake is one of the most recognizable figures in the world of skiing. Glen is credited as one of the pioneers of hotdogging, which is now officially recognized as the sport of "freestyle skiing". He became famous in the late 1980s when he featured in several ski movies, and continues to make regular appearances in ski magazines and at ski shows, as well as being an ambassador for Heavenly Ski Resort, Lake Tahoe (California). Glen is highly respected by skiers and snowboarders around the world for his dedication to the sport and for his active promotion of the ski lifestyle.

Text credits

Picture credits

All photographs supplied by Skishoot-Offshoot.

PHOTOGRAPHERS:
Page 5 Roger Rowland; **10–11** Ian Jones; **12** Stan Hill; **14–15** Ian Jones; **16** Tim Hall; **18–19** Duncan Walpole; **20–21** Doug Sager; **23** Ian Jones; **24–5** Sylvain Grandadam; **27** Adrian Myers; **28–9** Tim Hall; **30** Duncan Walpole; **32–3** Martin Hayhow; **34–5** Ann Gray; **37** Duncan Walpole; **38–9** Duncan Walpole; **40–41** Amanda Stokes; **42** Duncan Walpole; **44–5** Roger Rowland; **47** Don Cole Harvey; **48–9** Ian Jones; **50** Ian Jones; **53** Lucy Mason; **54–5** Gareth Williams; **56–7** John Chittin; **59** Ski Miguel; **60–61** Amanda Stokes; **63** Don Cole Harvey; **64–5** Peter Hardy; **66–7** Ian Jones; **68** Amanda Stokes; **70–71** John Chittin; **72–3** Toby Smedley; **74** Duncan Walpole; **76–7** Ian Jones; **78–9** Toby Smedley; **81** Don Cole Harvey; **82–3** Ian Jones; **84–5** Roger Rowland; **86** Don Cole Harvey; **88–9** Andrew Hendry; **91** Stan Hill; **92–3** J. Macpherson; **94–5** Don Cole Harvey; **96** Gareth Williams; **98–9** Don Cole Harvey; **101** Huber; **102–3** Andrew Hendry; **104** Luxo; **106** Duncan Walpole.